"Round the Twist"

Creative Cordmaking

by
Jacqui Carey

"OTT" Embellishment series - Book One.
Ideal for any textile enthusiast who wishes to
create complimentary embellishments.
Exploring simple yet effective techniques that
require little or no equipment.
"Round the Twist" looks at new ideas for
the simple twisted cord.

*Colour reproduction, design and photography by
Carey Company.
Printed by Brightsea Press Ltd, Exeter, U.K.
Published by Carey Company.
'Round the twist' title courtesy of Hester Pickles.*

ISBN: 0 9523225 3 6

'Twist and Fold' Method

The oldest example of a twisted cord dates back to 15,000 B.C. It is a basic technique, yet despite its age there still remains a wealth of untapped potential awaiting discovery.

This book looks at making twisted cords using a simple but effective method of twisting and folding.

'Twist and Fold' Method.

1. Select the threads you wish to use. In this example (Sample 1), 4 strands of knitting wool have been chosen.

2. Secure the ends of your threads to a fixed point. You can use sticky tape to attach the ends to a table. Or you can wrap the threads around a warping post. You can even try pinning the threads to your clothing ! (Note that the example around the post has been made from a single length of uncut thread that has been folded into four.)

3. Hold the free ends of your threads together and away from the fixed point so that they remain taut.

Sample 1.

4. Twist the threads. This example is twisted in a clockwise direction (to the right).

5. Continue holding the free ends in the right hand. With your left hand, hold the centre of the threads.

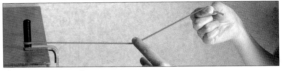

6. Keep the threads under tension (taut) whilst folding them in half so that the free ends meet the fixed point.

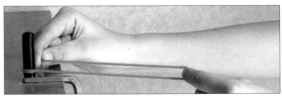

7. Keep holding the threads at both ends but allow the threads in the left hand to twist between your fingers. You can 'help' them by twisting in an anti-clockwise direction.

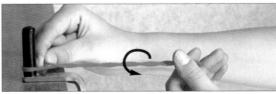

If you just let go - the threads will automatically twist themselves together. However, they can go a bit wild!

8. Remove the cord from your fixed point and secure the ends to prevent them from unravelling.

'Twist and Fold' Method

How much twist ?

You can control the amount of twist that is put into the cord. Look at the photo to see the difference it can make. A common mistake is to stop twisting too soon, this results in a slack cord. If you wish to be uniform in the twist, you can count the number of turns that you make.

The same cord with more twist (left) and less twist (right).

Securing ends.

You can temporarily tie the ends of the cord with a separate piece of thread or you can wrap them with a little sticky tape.

You may wish to try this Wall Knot, a traditional way of securing sailor's ropes. Other methods of securing are found on pages 22 and 23.

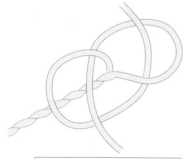

Wall Knot for Z-spun cords

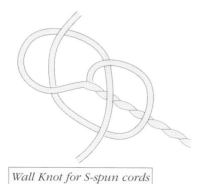

Wall Knot for S-spun cords

How long ?

The action of folding the thread in half immediately reduces the finished length of the cord. This is further reduced by the 'take-up' of the twist. So, to make a set length of cord you will need to use "twice as much and a little bit more". The amount of take up will vary depending on various factors, such as the quantity and type of thread and the amount of twist. However, as a rough guide, to produce 1 metre of cord you will need threads of about 2¼ metres in length.

The 'twist and fold' method is quick and simple as no equipment is required. However, if you want to produce large quantities, it can be a bit tedious to twist. You can push a stick or pencil between the threads to use as a 'handle' or to really speed things up attach the threads onto a hook in a hand drill !

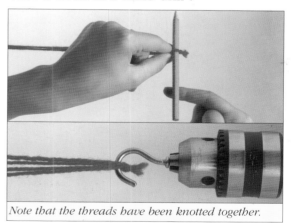

Note that the threads have been knotted together.

The 'twist and fold' method is only practical for making twisted cords up to 1.5 metres in finished length. This is because it is difficult to tension threads longer than your arm span, unless you have a friend to help !

The 'side-by-side' method described on page 24 is better for producing really long cords. On this page you will also find details of other gadgets used to produce twisted cords.

'S' and 'Z' Twist

One of the first things to consider is the difference between 'S' and 'Z' twisted threads. Twisting in a clockwise direction forms an S-twist whilst twisting in an anti-clockwise direction forms a Z-twist.

Look at a thread and mentally draw an 'S' and 'Z' over it. The central part of an 'S' lies from top left to bottom right and corresponds to the diagonal lines on an S-twist thread. The reverse is true of a Z-twist thread.

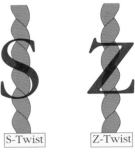

S-Twist   Z-Twist

When using the 'twist and fold' method shown on page 2, the action of folding reverses the twist so that when the threads are twisted clockwise (to the right) an S-twist is formed but when these are folded in half they create a Z-twist cord. When threads are twisted anti-clockwise (to the left) a Z-twist is formed but when these are folded in half they form an S-twist cord.

This may seem a trivial detail but as you will discover, different effects can be exploited by altering the way in which you use these S and Z-twists. For example just look at the difference between going 'with' the twist and going 'against' it.

Going 'with' the twist. (Sample 2)

1. Take 8 strands of Viscose (a Z-twist thread)

2. Secure the ends to a fixed point and twist the threads in an anti-clockwise direction (going 'with' the Z-twist of the thread).

3. Fold in half and allow the threads to twist, forming an S-twist cord.

Going 'against' the twist. (Sample 3)

1. Take 8 strands of Viscose (a Z-twist thread)

2. Secure the ends to a fixed point and twist the threads in a clockwise direction (going 'against' the Z-twist of the Viscose).

3. Fold in half and allow the threads to twist, forming a Z-twist cord.

Sample 2

Sample 3

Now compare the two samples. Going 'with' the twist produces a firmer, crisper result. Whilst the sample that goes 'against' the twist has slightly untwisted the Viscose to give a softer finish.

It is worth noting that you will always be able to go 'with' the twist. However, trying to go 'against' the twist of a single thread or cord will result in unravelling the original.

Wrapping

Sample 28 (page 12, left).
Make a cord from 2 strands of mauve Gimp twist-
ed anti-clockwise. Add this to 1 strand of Ruched
Ribbon and re-twist in a clockwise direction. Wrap
a black Gimp into each groove.

Sample 29 (page 12, right).
Make a cord from 8 strands of mauve Rayon Floss
twisted clockwise. Make another cord from 2
strands of mauve Gimp twisted clockwise. Join the
two cords together and re-twist in an anti-clock-
wise direction. Make another cord from 2 strands
of black Gimp and 4 strands of black Perle joined
end-to-end and twisted clockwise. Wrap this black
cord over the re-twisted cord in an anti-clockwise
direction so that it goes 'against' the spiral of the
grooves.

Sample 30 (page 13, left).
Make a cord from 10 strands of black Perle with
10 strands of burgundy Perle and twist clockwise.
Add this cord to 40 strands of Rayon Floss and re-
twist anti-clockwise. This is now wrapped with two
separate pre-made cords (one is made from a sin-
gle strand of Rayon Floss twisted in a clockwise
direction; the other is made from two strands of
Rayon Floss twisted clockwise).

Sample 31 (page 13, right).
Make a cord from 8 strands of pinky Rayon Floss
twisted clockwise. Add 60 strands of black Chenille
and re-twist in an anti-clockwise direction. Now
wrap a burgundy Russia Braid into each groove.

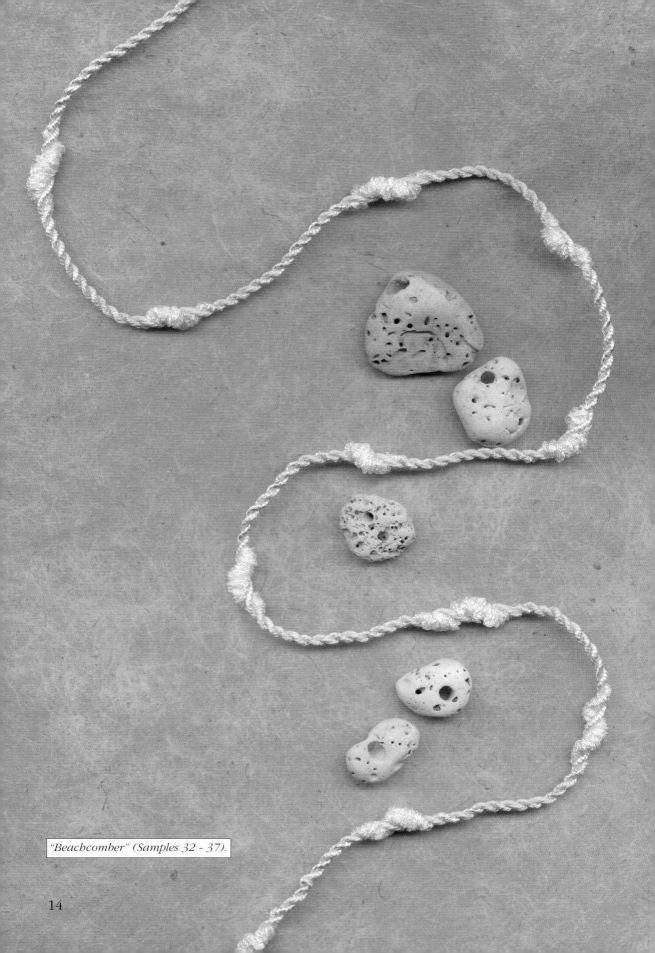

"Beachcomber" (Samples 32 - 37).

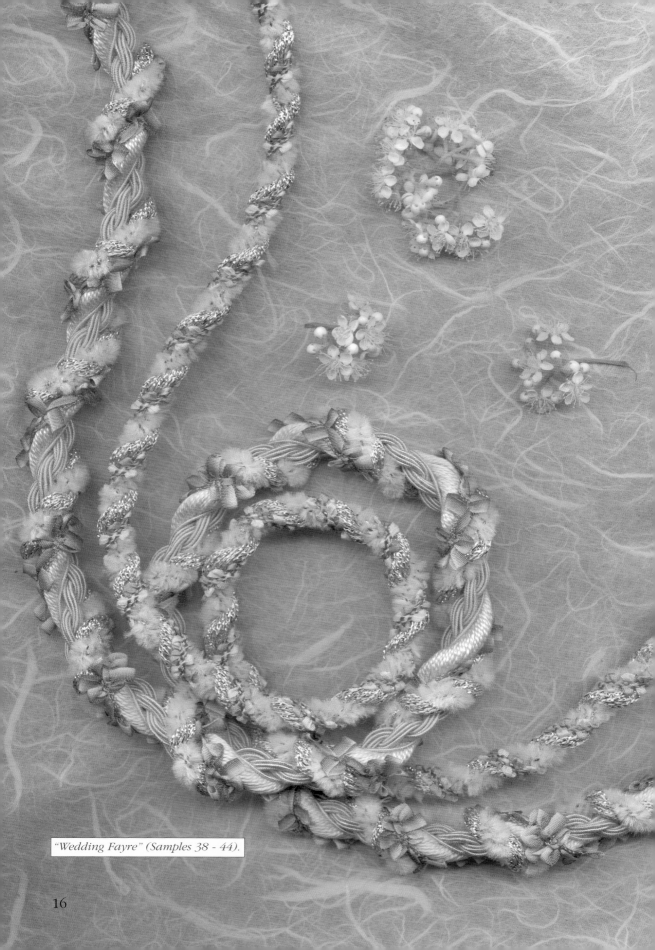

"Wedding Fayre" (Samples 38 - 44).

16

Samples

The samples shown in this book are life size and are used to illustrate ideas. The threads used to make these samples are shown on pages 26 and 27. Some of the fancy threads are made for the fashion market so they can vary in availability. However, all sorts of threads and fibres can be used. It is often a case of not what you use but how you use it !

So try out alternatives and experiment with new threads. Do not be disheartened if things do not look perfect first time. Keep samples and records and use these as a spring board for new ideas !

Sample 32.
Ruche some cream Knitting Ribbon to form a slubbed thread. Join this 'end-to-end with 4 strands of cream Perle and twist clockwise.

Sample 33.
Make a cord from 4 strands of Fancy Yarn 'Five' and 8 strands of cream Gimp joined 'end-to-end' and twisted clockwise. Add 60 strands of cream Perle and re-twist anti-clockwise.

Sample 34.
Make a cord from 4 strands of Fancy Yarn 'Five' and 8 strands of cream Gimp joined 'end-to-end' and twisted clockwise. Add 40 strands of Fancy Yarn 'Four' and re-twist anti-clockwise.

Samples

Sample 35.
Make two cords, each from 4 strands of Rayon Floss twisted anti-clockwise. Join both cords together and twist clockwise. Then add 6 strands of black Chenille and re-twist in an anti-clockwise direction.

Sample 36.
Make a cord from 8 strands of Fancy Yarn 'Five' and 16 strands of cream Gimp joined 'end-to-end' and twisted anti-clockwise.

Sample 37.
Make a cord from 4 strands of cream Gimp twisted clockwise. Join to 8 strands of cream Gimp and re-twist anti-clockwise. Join this cord to 80 strands of Fancy Yarn 'Four' and re-twist clockwise. Finally, wrap a Fancy Yarn 'Five' into one of the grooves.

Samples

Sample 38.
Make a cord from 8 strands of burgundy Stranded Cotton and 8 strands of pink Cotton Perle No5 joined 'end-to-end' and twisted clockwise. Make another cord from 4 strands of green Cotton Perle twisted clockwise. Join the two cords together 'end-to-end' and twist anti-clockwise.

Sample 39.
Make a cord from 16 strands of cream Glitter and 6 strands of Fancy Yarn 'One' joined 'end-to-end' and twisted clockwise. Wrap with a Fancy Ribbon 'One' into one of the grooves.

Sample 40.
Make a cord from 10 strands green Cotton Perle No5 twisted clockwise. Join 'end-to-end' with 20 strands of burgundy Stranded Cotton and re-twist anti-clockwise. Wrap this cord with a green Russia Braid in each groove. Then join 'end-to-end' with 40 strands of green Perle No5 and re-twist clockwise. Wrap this cord with a green Russia Braid in each groove.

Sample 41.
Make a cord of 8 strands of burgundy Stranded Cotton and 8 strands of green Perle joined 'end-to-end' and twisted clockwise. Add 30 strands of burgundy Stranded Cotton 'end-to-end' and re-twist anti-clockwise. Wrap a Fancy Ribbon 'One' into one of the grooves.

Samples

Sample 42.
Make a cord from 12 strands of burgundy Stranded Cotton and 12 strands of green Perle No5. joined 'end-to-end' and twisted clockwise. Join this to 24 strands of cream Perle and re-twist anti-clockwise. Wrap both grooves with a green Russia Braid.

Sample 43.
Make a cord from 8 strands of cream Gimp twisted anti-clockwise. Join this 'end-to-end' with 40 strands of cream Perle and re-twist clockwise. Wrap a cream Gimp into one groove. Into the other groove, wrap a pre-made cord (16 strands of cream Glitter and 6 strands of Fancy Yarn 'One' joined 'end-to-end' and twisted clockwise). Finally wrap a Fancy Ribbon 'Two' into the same groove so that it lies between the wrapped cord and the Perle.

Sample 44.
Make a cord from 12 strands of burgundy Stranded Cotton and 6 strands of pink Perle No5. joined 'end-to-end' and twisted clockwise. Join this to 12 strands of green Perle and re-twist anti-clockwise. Join this cord to 30 strands of green Perle and re-twist clockwise.
Now start a new cord. 'Parallel' join 8 strands of cream Perle and 8 strands of pink Perle and twist clockwise. Join this to another cord made from 8 strands of burgundy Stranded Cotton and 8 strands of green Perle twisted clockwise. Twist the two cords together in an anti-clockwise direction.
Finally, wrap the second cord into one groove of the first.

Ends and Joins

The ends of a twisted cord will start to unravel if they are not secured. Whipping the threads together will provide a neat and permanent fixing for your cords. It is possible to pinch the ends together in your fingers whilst you do this. However, it is much easier if you put a temporary tie in place just to help you at this point.

Permanent Whipping.

1. To whip the ends, take a needle and thread (something that compliments the cord). Sample 45 uses the same navy Perle that was used in the making of the cord.

2. Secure the thread into the cord with a couple of stitches. Note the temporary tie (red) stops the cord from unravelling.

3. Wrap the thread tightly around the cord. You can make as many or as few turns as you wish but try to keep the thread coiling neatly.

4. Secure the thread back into the cord with a couple more stitches and trim the thread end.

5. Remove the temporary tie and trim the ends of the cord to suit.

Sample 45. Make a cord from 6 strands of turquoise Viscose and 12 strands of navy Perle No5, joined 'end-to-end' and twisted clockwise. Join this to 24 strands of cream Perle No5 and re-twist anti-clockwise. Wrap a black Russia Braid into one groove and a blue Russia Braid into the other groove.
A permanent whipping is made near the end. The threads are then unraveled and steamed over a kettle before being trimmed into a tassel.

You can also make a join by whipping together both ends of the same cord (see photograph on opposite page).

Ends and Joins

Looped End.

It is possible to produce a cord with a neat loop at one end which will not unravel. Coloured threads joined 'parallel' (page 6) will automatically create this effect when the threads are folded in half at the centre. In contrast, the 'end-to-end' examples (page 7) will not. However, this can be resolved with a little forward planning.

Prepare your threads so that the 'end-to-end' join is formed with interlocking loops of thread as shown in the diagram (top right). Then continue to make the cord in the usual manner.

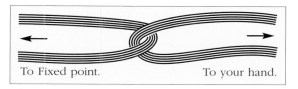

To Fixed point.　　　　　　　To your hand.

Looped Join.

The simplest way to join together the two ends of a cord (to make a bracelet or necklace) is to have a loop on one end and a knot on the other. The knot can then be pushed through the loop and the twist of the cord will hold the knot in place. A simple Overhand knot will suffice but a Double Overhand looks better.

Alternatively, instead of a knot you could sew a bead, button or toggle onto the end of the cord.

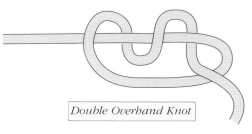

Double Overhand Knot

Sample 45 with both ends whipped together.

A blue and navy version of Sample 7 (page 7). The threads have been interlocked as shown in the diagram above so that they form a looped end. A Double Overhand knot has been tied in the other end so that the two ends can be connected together.

Cord Winders

Producing large quantities of twisted cord can be rather tedious. We have already seen that a pencil or a drill can be used to speed up the process. However, there are other machines and gadgets that have been developed especially for this purpose. Even Leonardo da Vinci had a go at designing one.

Most cord winders use a different approach to the 'twist and fold' method, although both methods can achieve the same results. Most cord winders start with the threads for both spirals lying separately, side-by-side to each other. These are then both twisted independently in the same direction before being twisted together in the opposite direction.

'Twist and Fold' method.   **'Side-by-Side' method.**

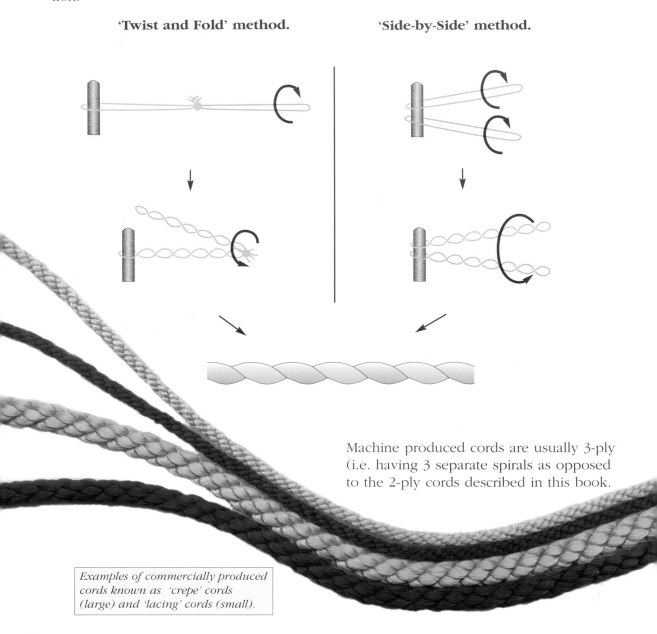

Machine produced cords are usually 3-ply (i.e. having 3 separate spirals as opposed to the 2-ply cords described in this book.

Examples of commercially produced cords known as 'crepe' cords (large) and 'lacing' cords (small).

Cord Winders

Hand held cord winder. Photo courtesy of Jennie Parry.

Spinning wheels can also be used to produce twisted cords.
Photo courtesy of M.J. Hutchins.

The Tibetan twister uses an ingenious technique based on a Tibetan spinning devise.
Photo courtesy of Ann Norman.

Materials

These threads are shown life size in order to give a guide to the materials used whilst making the samples in this book.

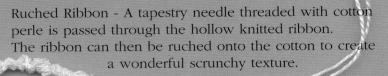

Ruched Ribbon - A tapestry needle threaded with cotton perle is passed through the hollow knitted ribbon. The ribbon can then be ruched onto the cotton to create a wonderful scrunchy texture.

Knitting Ribbon - a chainette tubular ribbon made from viscose.

Fancy Yarn 'One' - a double fringe of small tufts.

Fancy Yarn 'Two' - a double fringe of tufts.

Stranded Cotton - 6 strands of 'S' spun 2-ply, loosely 'Z' spun together.

Gimp - viscose whipped over a cotton core.

Viscose - a 2-ply, 'Z' spun filament fibre.

Glitter - a chained mix of lurex and viscose.

Cotton Perle No5 - a 2-ply, 'S' spun cotton.